The Blessing
Who May Ascend

Charles E. Jackson

THE BLESSING
Copyright © 2020 by Charles E. Jackson

All images presented herein are lawful protected by the owner of the copyright © Christopher A. Jackson. All rights related to these images are reserved and images presented here cannot be reproduced in any manner without the express written consent of the photographer.

All rights reserved. Neither this publication nor any part of this publication may be reproduced or transmitted in any form or by any means, electronic or mechanical, including photocopying, recording or any information storage and retrieval system, without permission in writing from the author.

Scripture quotations taken from the New American Standard Bible® (NASB), Copyright © 1960, 1962, 1963, 1968, 1971, 1972, 1973, 1975, 1977, 1995 by The Lockman Foundation. Used by permission. www.Lockman.org. Scripture quotations marked (NLT) are taken from the Holy Bible, New Living Translation, copyright ©1996, 2004, 2015 by Tyndale House Foundation. Used by permission of Tyndale House Publishers, a Division of Tyndale House Ministries, Carol Stream, Illinois 60188. All rights reserved. Scripture quotations marked (NIV) are taken from the Holy Bible, New International Version®, NIV®. Copyright © 1973, 1978, 1984, 2011 by Biblica, Inc.® Used by permission of Zondervan. All rights reserved worldwide. www.zondervan.com The "NIV" and "New International Version" are trademarks registered in the United States Patent and Trademark Office by Biblica, Inc.® Scripture quotations marked MSG are taken from THE MESSAGE, copyright © 1993, 2002, 2018 by Eugene H. Peterson. Used by permission of NavPress. All rights reserved. Represented by Tyndale House Publishers, a Division of Tyndale House Ministries. Scripture quotations marked (KJV) taken from the Holy Bible, King James Version, which is in the public domain.

Printed in Canada

Print ISBN: 978-1-4866-2086-9
eBook ISBN: 978-1-4866-2087-6

Word Alive Press
119 De Baets Street, Winnipeg, MB R2J 3R9
www.wordalivepress.ca

WORD ALIVE PRESS

FSC MIX Paper from responsible sources FSC® C103567

Cataloguing in Publication may be obtained through Library and Archives Canada

*For those along the Christian walk who have passed on the desire
to ascend into the hill of the Lord and receive a blessing.*

Contents

	Acknowledgements	vii
	Introduction	ix
1.	A Primer on Prayer	1
2.	What About Him or Her?	4
3.	What Is It Costing Us to Follow Christ?	7
4.	Forgiveness from Our Side	9
5.	Five Things People Blame the Church for But Shouldn't	11
6.	To Be a Saint	13
7.	The Way of Love	15
8.	Is Evangelism a Bad Word?	17
9.	The Complexion of the Church	19
10.	On Being Loved by God	21
11.	Jars of Clay	23
12.	When a Christian Sins Again	25
13.	Heaven as a Banquet	27
14.	Christmas Images	29
15.	Life Is Worth Living	31
16.	Not Ashamed	35
17.	A Family Together	38
18.	God's Care	40
19.	Why Repeat the Lord's Supper	42
20.	Christ Got Up, an Easter Reading	44

21.	Dialogue with Silence	46
22.	Readings on Healing and Forgiveness	48
23.	An Atheist Tells Us How to Win Others to Christ	51
24.	The Tradition of the Communion	53
25.	Beginning Thoughts on Communion	55
26.	Problems with Eating and Drinking the Elements	57
27.	Dry Bones, an Easter Story	60
28.	The Imitation of Christ	62
29.	Who to Choose	65
30.	Who May Ascend?	67
	Conclusion	71
	About the Author	73
	About the Photographer	75
	Index	77

Acknowledgements

Those who become serious writers, especially in the Christian religious scene, must be conscious of the multitude of those who have helped them along the way to publication.

I am grateful to the staff of Word Alive Press in Winnipeg for taking me on as a client for the third time. Thank you Evan, Ariana, Jen and your team for your professional expertise, especially during this stressful year of coping with the ongoing COVID – 19 pandemic.

Other pastors, churches and congregations have all had their influence in what is enacted week by week by way of sermons, pastoral care, visitation, and a variety of meetings – Baptists love meetings – and food! Most of what we do in and outside of the local church is unseen and anonymous as perhaps it should be, as done as unto the Lord Jesus and for the glory of God. But we are in the people business and need to insist on our gatherings as a part of God's will and purpose for his people.

My immediate family likewise deserves kudos for pushing me along to completion of the MS, "The Blessing – Who May Ascend?" These are by name: Dorothy – wife, Chris – son, Koula – daughter – in – law, Ruth – daughter, Rob – son – in – law, Ryan and Patrick – grandsons, Cassie – granddaughter, and two large grand dogs – Charlie & Maverick. Pancakes (with blueberries) and bacon breakfasts have become staples for our family gatherings at the lake. All of these have contributed to the "stuff" that is printed in this book, whether they have known it or not.

Lastly, as Paul wrote to the church at Philippi,

I thank my God in all my remembrance of you, always offering prayer with joy in my every prayer for you all, in view of your participation in the gospel from the first day until now. For I am confident of this very thing, that He who began a good work in you will perfect it until the day of Christ Jesus. (Phil. 1: 3 – 6)

Introduction

Are you close to God? Do you love the Lord Jesus Christ? Are you a spiritual person? Do you have a longing in your heart to know the Saviour better, and the Holy Spirit's gifts and graces more deeply? Are you where God wants you to be right now?

The title of this little book, *The Blessing: Who May Ascend?*, is meant to represent the climb, passage, or road taken by a worshipper of God to greater devotion or spiritual attainment in the Christian life.

The Old Testament symbolism of this metaphor can be found in Jacob's dream of a ladder set up between earth and heaven, with angels moving up and down upon it (Genesis 28:10–22). In this dream, God promises Jacob that the land where he lies will be given to him and his descendants, along with God's own presence and protection to fulfill the promise. Jacob returns his affirmation of the commitment with his own promise and calls the place Bethel, meaning House of God.

David, in Psalm 24, sees a similar ascent of worship. He writes of going up to Jerusalem in his own right as the king of Israel and appearing before God. Psalms 120–134 are likewise called psalms of ascent, to be sung by worshippers proceeding to Jerusalem to celebrate the designated feast days.

For the New Testament worshipper, an allusion of spiritual growth or ascendancy is given in the story of Mary and Martha, friends of Jesus (Luke 10:38–42). Traditionally, Martha has represented spiritual devotion by works, while Mary has represented worship by waiting—or the active way versus the quiet (passive) way.

The Christian mystics of the fourteenth century and onward sought to point the way to a closer walk with God, an ascent to the hill of the Lord (heaven). They spoke of seeking after God by various methods in order to achieve spiritual intimacy of the soul with God. But as one of their own cautioned,

> Since none can attain this blessed state, save those whom God himself leads and places therein, we do not pretend to introduce any into it, but only to point out the shortest and safest road that leads to it.[1]

---

[1] Fenelon, Mme. Guyon, and Molinos, *A Guide to True Peace, or the Excellency of Inward and Spiritual Prayer* (New York, NY: Harper and Brothers, 1946), 22–23.

The Blessing

It is hoped that this anthology of seemingly disconnected topics or essays will stimulate some souls to climb a little higher on the ladder of desire and love of our Saviour Jesus Christ.

It is our purpose to consider a pathway to God through the ministry of the Holy Spirit of our Lord Jesus, and a key requirement of this ascent must be its reference to the Bible along each step of the way. It is not just spiritual hunger we are after, but a heartfelt yearning for something more of God.

In the words of the poet Frederick William Faber:

'Tis not enough to save our souls,
To shun the eternal fires;
The thought of God will rouse the heart
To more sublime desires.

God only is the creature's home,
Though rough and straight the road;
Yet nothing less can satisfy
The love that longs for God…[2]

And when longing becomes desire, we find this is exactly what the Father wishes for us:

God loves to be longed for, He loves to be sought,
For He sought us Himself with such longing and love;
He died for desire of us, marvelous thought!
And He yearns for us now to be with Him above.[3]

---

[2] A.W. Tozer, *The Christian Book of Mystical Verse* (Harrisburg, PN: Christian Publications, 1963), 51. Quoting Frederick William Faber.

[3] Ibid., 57.

A Primer on Prayer

Chapter One

The Bible tells us that while Jesus was praying in the Garden of Gethsemane, and after He had finished one His disciples said to Him, *"Lord, teach us to pray just as John also taught his disciples"* (Luke 11:1; see also Luke 11:1–13). In this chapter, I offer a primer—or starting point—on prayer, which is a key to one's ascent in the Christian life. Notice what this disciple of Jesus did *not* ask for:

- Teach us to preach.
- Teach us how to work miracles.
- Teach us how to cast out demons.
- Teach us how to live a better life.
- Teach us how to have victory over sin.
- Teach us how to know Your will.

There is nothing wrong with any of the above prayers, but they don't come first.

Jesus also does not mention any negatives. He focuses on the positive answer, giving them the Lord's Prayer.

Then, to explain how Christians are to work this out in their daily lives, Jesus tells them a short story about a friend in need, introducing them to the little-known word *importunity*, which means "to harass with persistent demands or request… to ask or beg… to annoy."[4]

And to drive home the need further, Jesus gives the disciples a little formula:

- Ask to receive.
- Seek to find.
- Knock to open.

---

[4] Funk & Wagnalls, *Standard College Dictionary* (Toronto, ON: Fitzhenry & Whiteside, 1976), 675.

The Blessing

The tense is in the continuous present—to keep on asking, seeking, and knocking. Or, as the old-time preacher asked, "Are your knuckles bleeding yet?"

To emphasize the intensity and continuity of the prayer request, Jesus adds another short story in Luke 18:1–8 about the unbelieving judge who was asked to mete out justice to a woman. Jesus said, "Even though the judge didn't fear God or respect man, because she kept coming to him, bothering him, wearing him out, he decided to give her justice."

Notice that there is no time limit mentioned, nor does Jesus bring up the petitioner's unworthiness.

In both of these stories, Jesus's focus is on God's knowledge of a person's need and His gift of the Holy Spirit to answer the prayer with exactness.

For the Christian believer, this means:

- You don't need a theological degree to get answers to prayer.
- You don't need to perform an impossible feat of strength or spiritual discipline.
- You don't need to be an overachiever of any age, rank, or status.
- You just need to open the desire of your heart and words of your mouth and do what Jesus teaches in answer to the request: "Lord, teach us to pray."

Since this is only a primer on Christian prayer, the content of what we pray, when we pray, and how we pray can be left for other studies.

We now include the Lord's Prayer as left to us in a common rendering of the text of Matthew 6:9–13, and Luke 11:2–4, to be used either personally or in a worship service as part of the liturgy.

If you are unsure of starting with "Our Father," you can instead say "My Father." The Lord won't mind the intimacy!

Our Father who art in heaven,
Hallowed be thy name.
Thy kingdom come.
Thy will be done on earth, as it is in heaven.
Give us this day our daily bread.
And forgive us our trespasses,
As we forgive those who trespass against us.
And lead us not into temptation,
But deliver us from evil.
For thine is the kingdom,

And the power, and the glory,
For ever and ever. Amen.

As Dr. D. Martyn Lloyd-Jones assures us,

I have always been comforted by this thought, that whatever I forget in my own private prayers, as long as I pray the Lord's Prayer, I have at any rate covered all the principles.[5]

Mink (Psalm 16:11)

---

5   Dr. D. Martyn Lloyd-Jones, *Sermon on the Mount, Volume Two* (Downers Grove, IL: InterVarsity Press, 1960), 50.

What About Him or Her?
Chapter Two

As Jesus is about to depart and return to heaven, He gives final instructions to His disciples—in particular to Peter and John.[6]

Jesus reconfirms Peter in his faith by posing this threefold question: "Do you love me?" He then directs his vocation with a threefold affirmation: "Feed My sheep."

He then turns to John, whom He loved, and gave Him similar directions: "Follow Me!"

Peter becomes curious and wants to know if John is getting one up on him from Jesus. We might conclude that Peter is jealous of John.

Our lesson here is mixed and multiple:

1. Be cautious in judging and discerning someone else's will in life. You may be wrong! You may not know enough to be able to know for sure.
2. You may think and believe that you are better suited for a certain role than another. A prayer from John Baillie in confession may help: "My unwillingness to believe that thou hast called me to a small work and my brother to a great one: O Lord forgive."[7]
3. Jesus's answer for Peter is brief and curt: *"If I want him to remain [not die] until I come, what is that to you? You follow Me!"* (John 21:22) Jesus is telling Peter to mind his own business!

We need to be very careful about this. It takes spiritual maturity and a measure of giftedness to say to another, "I believe God wants you to do this or that with your life."

Consider the following examples.

Eric Liddell was a gold medallist in running at the 1924 Olympics in Paris. Following the Games, he was scheduled to travel to China as a missionary, but he was in love with a gifted artist named Eileen Sopher. She was germaphobe and

---

6   Read the full story in John 21.
7   John Baillie, *A Diary of Private Prayer* (London, UK: Oxford University Press, 1975), 15.

refused to go with him. Did he decide to stay? No. He said, "No, I will not stay here in Scotland. God wants me to go to China." And that is what he did![8]

Winston Churchill was prime minister of Great Britain when he faced his darkest hour during World War II. The king visited him and advised him to ask the people what to do. Churchill then went to an underground subway alone and asked a variety of the riders, to their astonishment:

Q: Do you want me to pursue terms of surrender? A. No.
Q. Do you want to see the swastika flying over Buckingham Palace and Parliament? A. No.
Q. Do you want me to leave 300,000 troops stranded at Dunkirk? A. No.

Winston then went back to Parliament and made his famous speech, "We shall never surrender…!" And the rest is history.

If the BEF (British Expeditionary Force) had been captured or destroyed at Dunkirk, Britain would almost certainly have been forced to surrender…
The sudden shock of Dunkirk was the spark for the creation of modern Britain.[9]

American painter Norman Rockwell once painted a picture of a cathedral in New York City showing crowds moving past with downcast eyes and hunched shoulders. The church's welcome sign shows the daily sermon's title: "Lift Up Thine Eyes."

Consider these guidelines for life:

- Don't look back.
- Don't look around.
- Keep your eyes on Jesus.
- Keep moving ahead.
- Do what is at hand.
- Do what you can.
- Do it to the end.

---

[8] Duncan Hamilton, *For the Glory: Olympic Legend Eric Liddell's Journey of Faith and Survival* (Toronto, ON: Penguin Random House, 2016), 129–142.

[9] Joshua Levine, *Dunkirk: The History Behind the Motion Picture* (New York, NY: HarperCollins, 2017), 300, 305.

The Blessing

    Here's a thought on the will of God. Let's take Romans 12:1–2 as a guide and consider the last clause: *"that you may prove what the will of God is, that which is good and acceptable and perfect"* (Romans 12:2)

    If it is not good and acceptable and perfect, it is not the will of God!

American Bittern (Proverbs 3:5–6).

What Is It Costing Us to Follow Christ?

Chapter Three

Many in our world, and even in the average church, live under the illusion that our lives are our own to utilize as we please. But as noted popular preacher Fred Craddock suggests:

> Some people think they can join a church and get close to Christ, and then pick and choose the things they like and discard the rest. Come now and then. Do a little now and then. Maybe serve on a committee now and then. Give a little now and then. Pour coffee and bring some cookies now and then. Compliment the pastor now and then. And then they die now and then, and hope for heaven now and then. Well maybe![10]

He then challenges us:

> I've had all that stuff that you do and talk about and threw it all away. I count it as loss. I dumped it overboard and threw it all in the garbage. I gave up my own agenda, my own pride, my own plans and took up Christ. I didn't add a little church or religion or faith as it might fit or not. This is the way I see it now, and I'm the first to confess that I'm not there yet. I haven't arrived. I'm not perfect. But think about it. If we are supposed to imitate Jesus and be like him; he put aside his royal and divine prerogatives and place. His was a downward mobility–humanness, emptiness, servant-hood, humility, obedience to death, death on a cross, - no rights, privileges or honors until after the cross and resurrection. What about our selfishness, our jealous independence, our calendar of activities in life? Paul had the idea that to follow Jesus meant to love, to care, to give, to serve, to suffer and to sacrifice if need be unto death.
>
> Are we missing something here? Paul's attitude is this: I want to have this, to lay hold of this, to press on to it, to forget the past and reach forward to this kind of life. I want this as my goal and prize. How about it?[11]

Is Craddock right in his summation of the reality in our churches today?

---

10 Fred Craddock, *The Cherry Log Sermons* (Louisville, KY: John Knox Press, 2001), 97.
11 Ibid.

The Blessing

Bishop William Willimon gives us an example of what our churches' message should be. We go to church to be reminded that the lives we live are not our own. When we grow up, we are asked to commit our lives to Christ and be baptized. We may sing, "Take my life and let it be consecrated, Lord, to thee." God doesn't accept our lives as much as he takes it, since our lives are His anyway!

As Willimon challenges us,

As his task requires, the bishop is often asked to deliver tough news to his area pastors. On one call he asked a pastor to move to another pastorate and take a seven thousand dollar cut in salary. The response was: "Bishop, there is no way they can hurt me financially as bad as Jesus hurt me when he called me into this ministry. I was pulling down eighty-five thousand a year when Jesus grabbed me and made me go to seminary.[12]

Is this too costly, too restrictive, or too narrow a pathway of obedience to Christ? Or is it the norm we have tragically fallen away from? What do you think?

Snowy Owl (Ephesians 2:8-9)

---

12   William H. Willimon, *Thank God It's Friday: Encountering the Seven Last Words from the Cross* (Nashville, TN: Abingdon Press, 2006), 70.

Forgiveness from Our Side
Chapter Four

Many people have difficulty forgiving those who have hurt or wounded them in some way. Here are some truths about forgiveness which are critical to remember.

Replaying and rehearsing events that have hurt or injured us makes it difficult to forgive and forget. It's like picking at a scab that has already healed over a wound. Forgiveness comes from the heart and will. We choose to forgive.

We may remember wrongs, our wounds may persist, and we may feel the pain of it. The apostle Paul wrote about the *"brand-marks of Jesus"* on his body from spiritual conflicts (Galatians 6:17). He also said that he suffered daily emotional trauma and anxiety about the churches he had planted and pastored (2 Corinthians 11:28–29). We are able to help the wounded by being a wounded healer ourselves.

Regrets may plague us as we think that others don't deserve our forgiveness. That may be true, but we are instructed, *"Never pay back evil for evil to anyone"* (Romans 12:17) Think about how much God has on us, yet we are still forgiven in Christ.

We are to forgive even if it isn't returned. We are not supposed to forgive as much as we have been forgiven. There are no conditions required.

Repeated sins against us require repeat forgiveness. As Jesus told Peter, *"I do not say to you, up to seven, but up to seventy times seven"* (Matthew 18:22).

Restoration may be required if there is a conviction to do so. Zacchaeus promised Jesus that he would give half of his wealth to the poor and four times whatever he had cheated anyone on their taxes (Luke 19:1–10).

Reform isn't a prerequisite to our forgiveness. We are to forgive, and God is to change people's lives. Forgiveness is unconditional. The people who have hurt us may never change!

The Christian is not to exact retaliation or punishment. We are not to seek revenge. God will pay people back (Romans 12:19). As our example, Jesus *"never sinned, nor ever deceived anyone. He did not retaliate when he was insulted, nor threaten revenge when he suffered. He left his case in the hands of God, who always judges fairly"* (1 Peter 2:22–23, NLT).

It is always the norm for a sinful brother or sister to return to the flock. Exclusion or excommunication is to be temporary. The church's mandate is to renew our fellowship and revive our relationships.

The Blessing

It may be necessary for us to remove ourselves from future harm, even if we do forgive the other person. Jesus didn't return to those who crucified Him; He returned to his friends.

Reciprocal forgiveness is the only condition attached to the Lord's Prayer (Matthew 6:14–15).

Reproving or disciplining other Christians must be done within the biblical model of Matthew 18:15–20.

The gospel's direction is always resurrection and new life. We must forgive.

At the other end of forgiveness, we must always remember that receiving forgiveness, from God's side, as Henri Nouwen reminds us, "requires a total willingness to let God be God and do all the healing, restoring, and renewing."[13]

Belted Kingfisher (Psalm 18:16)

---

13   Henri Nouwen, *The Return of the Prodigal Son* (Toronto, ON: Doubleday, 1992), 53.

Five Things People Blame the Church for But Shouldn't

Chapter Five

On his blog, writer Carey Nieuwhof wrote about five things people blame the church for but shouldn't:

1. The church didn't stop you from growing spiritually. I'm responsible for my spiritual growth…
2. The church didn't burn you out… I am responsible for my burnout. I pushed too hard for too long. I didn't deal with underlying issues. I burned myself out…
3. The church didn't make you cynical… You let your heart grow hard. You chose to believe certain things about people, about God, about life, and it built a crust around something that used to be alive and vibrant…
4. The church didn't cause your unforgiveness. It's easy to hold a grudge. Get hurt (and yes, I've been hurt by people in the church too) and hang onto it long enough, and grudges will form… I love how Mark Twain phrased it: "Forgiveness is the fragrance that the violet sheds on the heel that has crushed it."
5. The church didn't make you lose your faith… I'm far from perfect, that our church is not perfect, and that there never will be perfection on this side of heaven.[14]

Indeed, no one is perfect. We all make mistakes. We choose to give up and run away. I have to make a choice to believe when there are reasons not to, to love people who don't love me back, to forgive when it's easier not to, and to trust when there is cause not to.

The answer is to be a part of the solution. The church is Jesus's body, bride, and building. He loved it, gave His life for it, is building it, and will come for it. So get involved, join, serve, worship, give, and go. You can make the world a better place under God!

---

[14] Carey Nieuwhof, "Five Things People Blame the Church for but Shouldn't," *Carey Nieuwhof*. Date of access: October 6, 2020 (https://careynieuwhof.com/5-things-people-blame-the-church-for-but-shouldnt/).

The Blessing

Common Golden Eye (Psalm 17:8)

To Be a Saint
Chapter Six

Many people aren't sure what a saint is. Some think it's a very holy religious person, usually very old who is purported to have performed a miracle and has lived a good life filled with good works. This person is then canonized by the pope, usually several years after their death. Mother Teresa of Calcutta would be a modern example, who was canonized on September 4, 2016.

From the Protestant point of view, and according to Scripture, several writers call faithful and believing Jews in the Old Testament "saints," and Christians in the New Testament are addressed as "saints" as well.[15]

For writer Fred Buechner, being a saint involves nine movements:

1. Life is Movement—You have to keep moving on. In the words of a motto of a private boys school, "Come to this place, little boys, in order to become men."
2. Live with courage and self-restraint.
3. Live with hands stretched out both to give and to receive gladness.
4. Work and weep for the broken and suffering of the world.
5. To be strangely light of heart in the knowledge that there is something greater than the world that mends and renews.
6. To know joy. It is like the story of Jesus telling about the man finding a pearl of great price in a field and "in his joy" he sells all that he has to buy the field.
7. And there is the sense too that once we have glimpsed this kingdom (this pearl), so much more wonderful than anyone could have dared hope, so much more within the reach than anyone could have dreamed.
8. And there is the sense too that once we have glimpsed this kingdom, tasted this life, we understand that nothing else matters.

---

[15] These references can be found in Deuteronomy, the Psalms, Proverbs, Job, Daniel, Zechariah, Paul in several letters, Jude, and John in Revelation.

The Blessing

9. And if it is our purpose to become saints, we find that it is God's "unsecret" purpose to make us saints.[16]

Fred Buechner also whimsically writes,

Turn around and believe that the good news that we are loved is gooder than we ever dared hope, and that to believe in that good news, to live out of it and toward it, to be in love with that good news, is of all things in this world the gladdest thing of all.[17]

What then is a saint? According to Philip Yancey,

I like Reynolds Price's definition: someone who, however flawed, "leads us by example, almost never by words, to imagine the hardest thing of all: the seamless love of God for all creation, including ourselves."[18]

Common Merganser (Romans 8:28)

---

16 Fred Buechner, *The Magnificent Defeat* (San Francisco, CA: HarperCollins, 1966), 116–123.
17 Fred Buechner, *Secrets in the Dark: A Life in Sermons* (San Francisco, CA: HarperCollins, 2006), 161.
18 Philip Yancey, *Vanishing Grace: What Ever Happened to the Good News?* (Grand Rapids, MI: Zondervan, 2014), 71.

The Way of Love
Chapter Seven

Paul wrote to the Corinthian church in his first letter that *"love edifies"* (1 Corinthians 8:1). He quickly followed with these words: *"If anyone supposes that he knows anything, he has not yet known as he ought to know; but if anyone loves God, he is known by Him"* (1 Corinthians 8:2–3).

From these verses, we glean the following:

1. Love says, "Someone is watching." So be careful.
2. Love says, "I am my brother's keeper." The weakest link matters.
3. Love says, "For the sake of Christ, I won't wound, hurt, offend, or cause to stumble or be responsible for the fall of another."
4. Love says, "I am accountable."
5. Love says, "I may have to waive my rights sometimes."
6. Love says, "I am not number one."
7. Love says, "I must abstain and control myself."
8. John Wesley said, "Love God and do as you please." Therefore, if I truly love God, I will do only what pleases Him.
9. Love says, "I care for the peace, the building up of the body of Christ, the church, and the work of God. Therefore I can't be negative, destructive, or critical toward the church or other Christians."
10. Love says, "I may have to take the loss in some things and suck it up and have the buck stop at me."
11. Love says, "I am free and strong, but I must be an open window and not a closed door for others to see and enter and want to stay."
12. Love says, "I love Christ and know He loves me. Therefore, the love of Christ compels me, controls me, motivates me, and dictates my life and actions." See 2 Corinthians 5:14.
13. Love says, "I want to be like Christ—to think like Christ, act like Christ, love like Christ, and be with Christ."

The Blessing

Cooper's Hawk (Revelation 4:8)

Is Evangelism a Bad Word?
Chapter Eight

An article in the Acadia Divinity College magazine strikes a chord of concern for Christians striving to reach out to others with the gospel of Christ. In it, Drs. Stephen McMullin and Anna Robbins ask this question: is evangelism really a bad word, and are the churches in this country and around the world who are pursuing souls for Christ not fulfilling their mandate of the Great Commission, as stated by Jesus in Matthew 28:18–20?

The article sees evangelism in Canada in a sad condition and seeks to point out reasons for it. Here we summarize the key issues for thoughtful prayer and positive action:

1. People are uncomfortable about even using the word evangelism.
2. Most people don't come to faith by this means anymore.
3. Christians are embarrassed about sharing their faith.
4. Is it unethical to share with someone who already has a faith or religion?
5. Tolerance and relative truth are part of a liberal trend in the theology of many churches. Asking "Who knows?" is the same as saying "It doesn't matter what you believe or how you behave."
6. What right do we have to bother others who might say, "You can't say there is anything wrong with me" or "I ought to be anything that I'm not already." That's judgmental and colonialism.
7. Congregations are more concerned about survival than salvation, about recruitment and keeping the church plant going with the young and new givers instead of evangelism.
8. We need to get away from barriers and buildings and be open to refugees and immigrants through love and welcoming programs and activities.
9. The "All Welcome" sign doesn't work anymore.[19]

---

19 Dr. Stephen McMullin and Dr. Anna Robbins, "Is Evangelism a Bad Word?" *Acadia Divinity College Magazine.* Winter 2018, 3–6.

The Blessing

Note: A question for reflection to these disturbing facts could be, "Have we been doing it wrong all these years, or do we just need to be open to new ways and means of reaching people of this generation with the gospel and the love of Christ?"

Eastern Chipmunk (Psalm 3:3)

The Complexion of the Church

Chapter Nine

There are many different views of what the church is like or should be. What follows is a report from a pastor who led a variety of congregations over a number of years. His observations may not be completely agreed with, but they should nonetheless be challenging to consider.

1. The church that gave the most pleasure was the one with the most pain.
2. The church that made the most progress was the one that had nothing to lose.
3. The church that grew the most was the one that gave the most.
4. The church that had the greatest resources was the stingiest.
5. The church that boasted the most gifts caused the most grief.
6. The church that had the most respect for their pastor never hurt their pastor.
7. The church that was the most troubled thought it was most true to the Bible.
8. The church that stressed holiness of life was the healthiest.
9. The church that was the greatest blessing was also the one that had been broken.
10. The church that risked was the church that reaped.

In fact, when you think about it, many of these observations sound very… well, New Testament and Pauline!

The Blessing

Four-Spotted Skimmer (Galatians 6:9)

On Being Loved by God
Chapter Ten

In his book, *Searching for God Knows What*, author Donald Miller shares three short stories about being loved by God. Toni Morrison a Nobel-prize-winning author, when asked why she had become such a great writer, said, "When I was a little girl and walked into a room where my father was sitting, his eyes would light up."[20]

Maya Angelou was once asked how she became such a popular writer after a horrifying childhood. She explained that while walking down the street with her mother one day, her mother stopped and said to her, "Baby, you know something? I think you are the greatest woman I have ever met."[21]

Boarding the streetcar, Maya thought to herself, "Suppose I really am somebody."[22]

Don Miller also writes about pulling a friend out of a proverbial closet where he'd been hiding. This friend was a hopeless alcoholic, his marriage was falling apart, his kids had been sent away, and he was suicidal. Miller talked him into entering a rehab program.

After two months of painful recovery, this man was asked how he was turning his life around. He answered that his father had flown in and attended a session during which each participant confessed his failings, weaknesses, and issues. When this man had finished speaking, his father stood up and said to the group, "I have never loved my son as much as I do at this moment. I love him, I want all of you to know I love him."[23]

At that moment, for the very first time, this friend was able to believe that God loved him, too.

In his gospel, John refers to himself five times as "the apostle whom Jesus loved." Imagine what that knowledge meant to John and how it would have carried him into old age and his exile on the Isle of Patmos where he wrote the Revelation.

Do you know that God loves you—all of you, in whatever state or condition you are in? Jesus loves you and died for His love of you. His Holy Spirit loves you and is trying to bring you back to His heart of love. Will you accept it

---

20 Donald Miller, *Searching for God Knows What* (Nashville, TN: Thomas Nelson, 2004), 128–131.
21 Ibid.
22 Ibid.
23 Ibid.

The Blessing

and allow Him to love you, heal you, save you, bless you, and use you for His glory? Do it now by faith and confession and commitment. Do it now!

Great Blue Heron (Psalm 148:10)

Jars of Clay

Chapter Eleven

But we have this treasure in jars of clay to show that this all-surpassing power is from God and not from us.

—2 Corinthians 4:7, NIV

Many years ago, I heard a speaker who focused on this scripture passage and related it to the Christian experience, wherein we contain Christ as a treasure to pass on to others. He made three solid points, and I've added a fourth of my own.

1. We are to contain, but not to originate. As the apostle Paul strongly asserted to the Galatians,

For I would have you know, brethren, that the gospel which was preached by me is not according to man. For I neither received it from man, nor was I taught it, but I received it through a revelation of Jesus Christ.

—Galatians 1:11–12

Christians have a precious and wonderful gift entrusted to them by the Holy Spirit. We don't have to dig around for some unknown truth. We have it within us! It is *"Christ in you, the hope of glory"* (Colossians 1:27). This treasure is about Jesus, *"who gave Himself for our sins so that He might rescue us from this present evil age, according to the will of our God and Father"* (Galatians 1:4).

This is an amazing truth. We must think of our human vessels as jars of clay which have leaks and cracks, breaks and flaws, and yet they are able to contain God!

2. We are to preserve, but not to contaminate. We are not to hang onto this gospel selfishly. We are not to add anything to it, take anything away from it, or water it down. Instead we are to hold it as our core faith and truth.

In older times, families used to preserve produce from their gardens in mason jars with appropriate preserving ingredients. These preserves were kept for several months, usually through the winter, and then used in the spring. One of the key requirements was to maintain the contents of these jars until they were needed.

The Blessing

That was the problem Paul had with the Galatian church. They were contaminating the gospel with other ingredients, just as he had found with the Corinthian church: *"But I am afraid that, as the serpent deceived Eve by his craftiness, your minds will be led astray from the simplicity and purity of devotion to Christ"* (2 Corinthians 11:3).

3. We are to transport, but not to stagnate. Jesus had a jar of clay as His human body—fragile, limited, tempted, tried, tested, and finally taken to the cross to die.

Jesus knew He was to give His life for the sins of the world and told His disciples this many times. Just as He broke the bread, just as the wine was poured out and consumed to the end, Jesus had nowhere to rest his head until he would say his last words on the cross: *"It is finished!"* (John 19:30)

We need to share the gospel with others, to get it out and move it along—to transport it. This is the Great Commission (Matthew 28:18–20).

4. We are to be made over, but not discarded. In a beautiful passage in Jeremiah 18:1–6, God presents the image of a clay pot being made on the wheel. This pot then becomes spoiled in the hand of the potter. But instead of discarding it as useless, the potter remakes it as it pleases him.

God likens this to His action in the life of His people when they sin and rebel against Him. God's ultimate purpose is to build up and to plant, not to pull down and destroy. Can we not see this as His purpose in the life of the church, the ministry and mission of Jesus, and the Holy Spirit in our own lives? (Matthew 16:18)

Twelve-Spotted Skimmer (Job 19:25)

When a Christian Sins Again
Chapter Twelve

Many Christians have difficulty sorting out what to do when they sin repeatedly, and aren't able to overcome those sins and therefore need constant or repetitive confession. If this is you, hear this wise counsel from spiritual directors of the church from another age:

From Father John of the Greek church:

When praying at night, do not forget to confess with all importunity, and sincerity and contrition, those sins into which you have fallen during the past day. A few moments of importunate repentance, before you sleep, and you will be cleansed from all your iniquity. You will be made whiter than snow. You will be covered with the robe of Christ's righteousness, and again united to Him.[24]

From St. Teresa of Avila:

Never mind who cries shame says our Lord to us. Keep on knocking, shame or no shame. "Think shame woman!" The devil said to St. Teresa. "A woman at your time of life having to make such a confession. And presumptuously hoping for pardon for such shameless sins. Think shame! Or if you will still presume to pray for forgiveness, at any rate wait a little. Do not go to God and you still reeking with such uncleanness. Wash in the holy water first. Perform a time of penance first…

The devil never so nearly had my soul forever, as just after another fall of mine, and when he cried, For shame, O woman, for shame…

---

[24] Alexander Whyte, *Bible Characters, Volume Two* (Grand Rapids, MI: Zondervan, 1952), 355.

The Blessing

> Never let anyone leave off prayer on any pretense whatsoever; great sins committed, or any pretense whatsoever… I tell you again that the leaving off prayer after sin was the most devilish temptation I was ever met with.[25]

As a habit, when beginning my personal prayer time, I use these three sentences as an introduction:

1. Lord Jesus Christ, Son of the living God, have mercy upon me, a sinner…
2. Lord Jesus Christ, Son of the living God, have mercy upon me, the chief of sinners…
3. Lord Jesus Christ, Son of the living God, have mercy upon me, the only sinner…

I've found that these centre my thoughts, humble my heart, and position me where I belong before God—on my knees.

Hooded Merganser (Ecclesiastes 3:1)

---

25   Ibid., 354.

Heaven as a Banquet
Chapter Thirteen

Gary Black Jr., author of *Preparing for Heaven*, spent several weeks at the bedside of Dallas Willard before he died. In his book, he imagined this picture of heaven, which seemed to be a colourful and hopeful encouragement for those who are suffering. It has been read at the beginning of Communion services:

> I imagine such a banquet will take a lot of planning, eons of forethought, boundless energy, and amazing levels of devotion. Such a banquet will perfectly quench every possible hunger and thirst.
>
> The triune God, the celebration's most glorious participant, will sit at the head of this table. He will offer his blessing. We will radiate his glory, as we finally behold him face-to-face. Every longing will cease, for we are wanted and honored around the table. There is a place setting for each of us. Most of us will likely have travelled long distances, and there will be amazing stories to tell. Old friendships and crucial relationships will be restored and redeemed. Faith will fill every cup. Hope will be the music carried in the air, and love's aroma will fill the room as it is lavishly served, one to another.
>
> We will experience eternal belonging. We will listen as the elders retell the story of God's glorious deeds, those known and unknown to us. We will serve others while being served by others. We will be delighted in while being delightful. We will celebrate while being a part of the celebration. We will be thankful, restful, and peaceful, all at once.
>
> I've started to pack away these invaluable treasures. I'm preparing my life, heart, mind, and soul, for eternal living. I'm endeavoring, with both setbacks and successes, to experience and instill the Fruit of the Spirit into my soul in a way that will make my life in the Kingdom of Heaven blessed, both now and throughout all eternity. I'm also making plans to be at the heavenly banquet table. I wouldn't miss it for anything.[26]

---

[26] Gary Black Jr., *Preparing for Heaven: What Dallas Willard Taught Me About Loving, Dying, and Eternal Life* (New York, NY: HarperCollins, 2015), 269.

The Blessing

Here is a bonus piece of writing for your blessing, from Mark Rutland:

By survey, the three words people would most like to hear are: I love you, I forgive you, and Supper's ready.[27]

Jesus says these things to us today!

Horned Grebe (Philippians 1:6)

---

27   Mark Rutland, *Streams of Mercy: Receiving and Reflecting God's Grace* (Ann Arbor, MI: Vine, 1999), 39.

Christmas Images

Chapter Fourteen

Thanks be to God for His indescribable gift!

—2 Corinthians 9:15

During the advent season, as we think of Jesus being born, we must also think of Him crucified, dead, buried, raised from the dead, and coming again. Charles Dickens wrote about this in a piece entitled *A Christmas Tree*, in 1850:

> What images do I associate with the Christmas music as I see them set forth on the Christmas Tree? Known before all the others, keeping far apart from all the others, they gather round my little bed. An angel, speaking to a group of shepherds in a field; some travellers, with eyes uplifted, following a star; a baby in a manger; a child in a spacious temple, talking with grave men; a solemn figure, with a mild and beautiful face, raising a dead girl by the hand; again, near a city gate, calling back the son of a widow, on his bier, to life; a crowd of people looking through the opened roof of a chamber where he sits, and letting down a sick person on a bed, with ropes; the same, in a tempest, walking on the water to a ship; again, on a sea-shore, teaching a great multitude; again, with a child upon his knee, and other children round; again, restoring sight to the blind, speech to the dumb, hearing to the deaf, health to the sick, strength to the lame, knowledge to the ignorant; again, dying upon a Cross, watched by armed soldiers, a thick darkness coming on, the earth beginning to shake, and only one voice heard, "Forgive them, for they know not what they do."…
>
> Now, the tree is decorated with bright merriment, and song, and dance, and cheerfulness. And they are welcome. Innocent and welcome be they ever held, beneath the branches of the Christmas Tree, which cast no gloomy shadow! But, as it sinks into the ground, I hear a whisper going through the leaves. "This, in commemoration of the law of love and kindness, mercy and compassion. This, in remembrance of Me!"[28]

---

28 Charles Dickens, "A Christmas Tree," *Gutenberg.org*. Date of access: October 6, 2020 (https://www.gutenberg.org/files/1467/1467-h/1467-h.htm).

The Blessing

Snowy Owl (Psalm 31:24)

Life Is Worth Living
Chapter Fifteen

Neil Postman, American educator and mass media critic, once asked two questions about the scientific view of the world:

> To the question, "How did it all begin?", science answers, "Probably by an accident." To the question, "How will it all end?", science answers, "Probably by accident." And to many people, the accidental life is not worth living.[29]

The Christian answer to these questions is that life is worth living because God has a word at the beginning, the middle, and the end of life—and there is no accident!

A Creation Word

The Christian Bible begins with these words: *"In the beginning God created the heavens and the earth"* (Genesis 1:1). No explanation of this statement is provided, except the actual carrying out of that created order through the next two chapters. There is no "probably by accident" explanation here.

It is assumed throughout the Old and New Testaments that if God is sovereign enough and omniscient enough and omnipotent enough, He is able to will whatever He wishes, and it is done either instantly by Him or by the process of an order issued by Him.

In a plainer and simpler rendering, the apostle Paul points to Jesus Christ as the source of all creation:

---

[29] John Eldredge, *Epic: The Story God Is Telling and the Role that Is Yours to Play* (Nashville, TN: Thomas Nelson, 2004), 9. Quoting Neil Postman.

The Blessing

> *He [Jesus] is the image of the invisible God, the firstborn of all creation. For by Him all things were created, both in the heavens and on earth, visible and invisible, whether thrones or dominions or rulers or authorities—all things have been created through Him and for Him. He is before all things, and in Him all things hold together.*
>
> —Colossians 1:15–17

The Old Testament prophet Jeremiah echoes the same message, that God is the initiator and sustainer of all things:

> *It is He who made the earth by His power, who established the world by His wisdom; and by His understanding He has stretched out the heavens.*
>
> —Jeremiah 10:12

Similar passages from the Psalms, Proverbs, Job, Isaiah, John, Hebrews, and 1 John confirm the creator's action through the Son.

> *…whom He appointed heir of all things, through whom also He made the world. And He is the radiance of His glory and the exact representation of His nature, and upholds all things by the word of His power.*
>
> —Hebrews 1:2–3

Since the Hubble telescope was launched in 1990, it has revealed to us amazing pictures of what the universe is really like, as well as how much we don't know about it thirty years later.[30]

Maybe God still has some secrets to show us!

A Continuing Word

Again, the apostle Paul gives us some deep theological statements on this issue:

> *And we know that God causes all things to work together for good to those who love God, to those who are called according to His purpose. For those whom He foreknew, He also predestined to become conformed to the image of His Son, so that He would be the firstborn among many brethren; and these whom He predestined, He also called; and these whom He called, He also justified; and these whom He justified, He also glorified.*

---

[30] "Hubble's Heavenly Visions," *National Geographic*. May 2020, 8–14.

What then shall we say to these things? If God is for us, who is against us?

—Romans 8:28–31

Here we have, in just a few sentences, God giving us His word that carries through life and into eternity. Or, as it has been said of the providence of God, we see the hand of God in the glove of history. Again, this is life with no accident.

A Concluding Word

The apostle Paul gives us a concluding word assuring us that life is not accidental, that there is a plan and purpose, and that there will be a final judgment based on every man's association with Jesus Christ. To the inquiring Greek philosophers, Paul was clear in his teaching about God and Jesus:

- God made the world and all things in it.
- He gives to us life and breath and all things.
- He made the nations of mankind and determined their times and boundaries and habitation.
- God is not far off, but near, and in Him we live and move and exist. Indeed, mankind is His offspring.
- He has fixed a day when He will judge the world through a Man whom He has appointed, proving it by raising Him from the dead. Jesus Christ is the Man!
- This resurrection teaching produced a mixed response.[31]

Whether or not the Athenians responded positively to Paul's preaching, these writings drive home the message that life is not accidental, concluding with oblivion. Rather, it is purposeful and meaningful, ordained and directed by God for His glory and our good.

As Paul affirmed this from beginning to end:

For I am confident of this very thing, that He who began a good work in you will perfect it until the day of Christ Jesus.

—Philippians 1:6

There it is—His word above all others. It is no accident!

---

[31] See Acts 17:24–34.

The Blessing

Leopard Frog (Hebrews 11:1)

Not Ashamed
Chapter Sixteen

For I am not ashamed of the gospel, for it is the power of God for salvation to everyone who believes, to the Jew first and also to the Greek.

—Romans 1:16

The apostle Paul wrote these words to the church at Rome. This followed his dramatic conversion to faith in the Lord Jesus Christ and continued through his journeys in Europe.

Here's a question: would we be ashamed to say that we were proud to be Canadians, or ashamed of our roots from some other place or background—our heritage, our home?

The apostle was so convinced that the gospel of Jesus—the truth of Him dying for our sins on the cross and providing a place for every believer in heaven—that he was willing to preach to anyone he met the unsearchable truth that had changed his life.

The following are just a few examples of those who changed their world and ours by not being ashamed!

Augustine. Until the summer of 386 A.D., Aurelius Augustine of North Africa had lived a wasteful youth to the sorrow of his godly mother. His soul was in distress as he searched for God.

He then heard a voice say to him, "Take up and read." He opened the Bible and read from Romans 13:13–14, where it says,

Let us behave decently, as in the daytime, not in carousing and drunkenness, not in sexual immorality and debauchery, not in dissension and jealousy. Rather, clothe yourselves with the Lord Jesus Christ, and do not think about how to gratify the desires of the flesh. (NIV)

The Blessing

This was his experience: "a clear light flooded my heart and all the darkness of doubt vanished away."[32] Augustine became one of the most important theologians and teachers and leaders of the church for a thousand years.

Martin Luther. In November 1515, Martin Luther, a German professor and doctor of theology, was struggling with the question of how to become right with God. While studying Romans, he read as if for the first time: *"But the righteous will live by faith"* (Romans 1:17).

He wrote, "I felt myself to be reborn and to have gone through open doors into paradise."[33] Through this experience, the Protestant Reformation was born and spread throughout the world.

John Wesley. On May 24, 1738, John Wesley, already a Church of England clergyman and missionary to the new world, went very unwillingly to a reading of Martin Luther's *Preface to the Book of Romans*. He writes,

> About a quarter before nine, while describing the change which God works in the heart through faith in Christ, I felt my own heart strangely warmed. I felt I did trust in Christ alone, for salvation; and an assurance was given me, that he had taken away my sins, even mine…[34]

Wesley became the founder of the Methodist movement, which changed much of the religious world of his day and our own.

Blaise Pascal. Blaise Pascal was a brilliant French mathematician from the seventeenth century. Upon his death, there was discovered stitched into his coat the following testimony:

MEMORIAL

The year of grace 1654. Monday, 23 November…From about half past ten in the evening until about half past midnight,

FIRE

"GOD of Abraham, GOD of Isaac, GOD of Jacob" not of the philosophers and of the learned.

Certitude. Certitude. Feeling. Joy. Peace. GOD of Jesus Christ.

"My God and your God…"

---

32   Father Carota, "St. Augustine, Great Sinner Turned Great Saint," *Traditional Catholic Priest*. August 28, 2014 (http://www.traditionalcatholicpriest.com/2014/08/28/st-augustine-great-sinner-turn-great-saint/).

33   Jim NcNeely, "Martin Luther's Conversion," *Therefore Now*. November 12, 2010 (https://thereforenow.com/2010/11/martin-luthers-conversion/).

34   Eugene Ikechukwu Ukaoha, "The Tenets of Wesley: An Evangelical Revival in Mainline Protestant Churches in Nigeria," *University of Nigeria Virtual Library*. Date of access: October 13, 2020 (http://www.unn.edu.ng/publications/files/Wesley%20Evangelical%20Revival%20and%20the%20Protestant%20Churches%20in%20Nigeria.%20-%20Print%20copy.docx1_.pdf).

> Forgetfulness of the world and of everything,
> Except GOD.
> He is to be found only in the ways taught in the Gospels.[35]

This mystical experience, along with his defence of the faith in the Pensées (Thoughts), confirms Pascal as an important figure in the rise and growth of the faith in Europe. He also invented the first calculator.

Let us conclude this chapter with the following hymn, "Ashamed of Jesus":

Jesus, and shall it ever be, a mortal man ashamed of thee?
Ashamed of thee whom angels praise, whose glories shine through endless days.
Ashamed of Jesus! That dear friend, on whom my hopes of heaven depend!
No, when I blush, be this my shame, that I no more revere his name.
Ashamed of Jesus! Yes, I may, when I've no guilt to wash away;
No tear to wipe, no good to crave, no fears to quell, no soul to save.[36]

Alaskan Black Bear (Psalm 104:25)

---

35 Brian McLaren, *A Generous Orthodoxy* (Grand Rapids, MI: Zondervan, 2004), 147–148.
36 Joseph Griggs, "Ashamed of Jesus," *Inspiring Hymns* (Grand Rapids, MI: Zondervan, 1965), #244.

A Family Together
Chapter Seventeen

As we come to the table of the Lord, we come to Christ for cleansing, forgiveness, renewal, restoration, revival, and recruitment for service. We are again to reorder our lives, start over, set new priorities, and put God and Christ first. We are, in a sense, told to go from the table and:

- Try to stay clean in a dirty world.
- Try to stay out of trouble in a troubled world.
- Try not to fall into the briers, stay out of the ditches, and not get drowned.
- Try not to get lost and watch out for the big bad wolf!

But if we do get lost, naturally wandering away like the one sheep, or the lost coin that slipping off the table, or the lost son who wastes his father's gifts, or the elder brother who sulks at home because he doesn't get the attention he thinks he deserves, what can we expect from a loving Father, a sacrificing Saviour, and a sweet and tender Holy Spirit?

Are you ready for this?

Consider the love of God—it is a seeking love, longing love, praying love, waiting love, running love, forgiving love, hugging love, kissing love, accepting love, welcoming love, lavishing love, party love, rejoicing love, inclusive love, sharing love, and eternal love.

Do you need anything like this today, right now? Take it by faith. It's yours.

As you come to the table of the Lord today at His invitation, are you ready for confession and forgiveness, for acceptance and a new start?

Do what you need to do now. Forget yesterday. Tomorrow hasn't come yet. Jesus is the same right now. Remember: your past is not your future!

Take and eat, and drink and remember what Jesus has done for you. Go in peace and serve Him. And be thankful.

Think of this example from Jan, the wife of Eugene Peterson, author of The Message translation of the Bible. While speaking to a group of women in Texas, she was asked, "Do you have any pearls of wisdom that you can give us for raising our children?"[37]

She answered, "Yes. Have a family meal together every evening!"[38]

The women were shocked by her answer, but dinner is a time for the entire family to come together. They pass and receive and tell stories while sharing potatoes, carrots, meat, dessert, coffee/tea, and juice. They can have a conversation, listen, be a blessing to each other, and give thanks.

But how many out of thirty-eight women did this? None! Upon hearing this, she was depressed for three weeks.

This is what Jesus did around Galilee for three years. He ate meals with people—sometimes even with the wrong kind of people. He scattered seed around for others to plant and harvest at maturity.

This is a meal today, and Jesus wants to share it with us. How about it?

Red Fox (Matthew 8:20)

---

37   Eugene Peterson, *The Pastor: A Memoir* (New York, NY: HarperCollins, 2011), 195.
38   Ibid.

God's Care
Chapter Eighteen

I penned the following poem spur of the moment while serving as a chaplain in a long-term care facility. While serving there, I experienced an almost daily loss of life brought on by a vicious virus. It seemed to bring some hope and comfort to those who read it:

> Is God with you when you sleep, when you can't, and when you weep?
> Is God with you when you walk on grass, when you shop at the mall, or only wish–and can't?
> Is God with you when you're alone, or with family and friends, or on the telephone?
> Is God with you when you have doubts, when your pains flair up, or you struggle with gout?
> Is God with you when you are small, when you're all grown up, or life has grown dull?
> If you've said yes to all of these things; your both alive and well and everything.
> But God is with you whether you know it or not, he's watching over you, at each turn and in each thought.
> So don't despair thinking God doesn't care, remember our Lord's footsteps in the sand pressed down more deeply when he took your hand.
> His love on the cross was clearly displayed, and even Jesus asked "Why?" before they took him away.
> Don't lose hope, he's preparing the way, for a fuller life and a better day.
> Soon enough the gloom will pass, the bad will be gone and the glory last.
> God wants you to know that he still cares, that Jesus is coming, so we better prepare.
> The angels are ready for the trumpet sound, for the signs to follow and Jesus' call.
> It's as close as if it were next door, when our body is changed, and we'll be free to soar.
> So get stripped down and be ready to go, let go of the baggage, 'cause your almost home.
> We may even be gone before we die!
> He'll be coming for you in the blink of an eye.

Northern Saw-Whet Owl (Psalm 104:12)

Why Repeat the Lord's Supper

Chapter Nineteen

The question is often asked, "Why do we repeat the Lord's Supper every month in most churches?" Think about the following reasons.

One, because even though Jesus has gone to heaven and by position and spiritually we are already with Him (Ephesians 2:6–7, Colossians 3:1, Romans 8:30), we are not there yet with Him in the body. Even at death, when we are *"absent from the body and… at home with the Lord"* (2 Corinthians 5:8), it is not clear what our state and condition is (1 John 3:2).

Therefore we need to be encouraged to hold fast, stand firm, and be strong and courageous in the faith and spiritual fight while we are still in the body. The Lord's Supper reminds us of this!

Two, because we still need to fight our enemies, the world, the flesh, and the devil with the weapons of prayer, the Holy Spirit's power, the fellowship of God's people, worship, the Word of God, and the visible elements of bread and the cup. There are some Christians who celebrate the Lord's Supper quarterly, weekly, and even daily.

Three, because even though we may feel unworthy to partake because of some sin of thought, word, or deed we've committed since our last service, Jesus still invites us, *"For as often as you eat this bread and drink the cup, you proclaim the Lord's death until He comes"* (1 Corinthians 11:26). It is a reminder that our sins are forgiven.

Think of those who were with the Lord at the initiation of the first Supper—Judas who betrayed Jesus, Peter who denied him three times, and they all forsook him and fled! Only John appears at the cross, and then it was to take Jesus's mother Mary home with him.

As the psalmist also reminds us, *"If thou, Lord, shouldst mark iniquities, O Lord, who shall stand? But there is forgiveness with thee, that thou mayest be feared"* (Psalm 130:3–4, KJV). There can never be a time on this side of heaven when forgiveness is not needed!

But the beloved apostle John assures us, *"If we confess our sins, He is faithful and righteous to forgive us our sins and to cleanse us from all unrighteousness"* (1 John 1:9). This is needed, even if we aren't conscious or aware of sin, which needs to be confessed and forgiven.

Why Repeat the Lord's Supper

And finally, because while we are still in the flesh we see through a glass darkly a reflection of the real, and know only in part until the great day of our Lord's return. So remember that no eye has seen, nor ear has heard, nor mind conceived, what God has prepared for those who love Him. The Supper is a peak, a glimpse, a foretaste of what is to come.

The apostle Paul tells us that the Holy Spirit interprets all of this to us (1 Corinthians 2:9–13). And we remember, give thanks, and partake of the Lord's Supper in faith. Amen.

Osprey (Psalm 104:17)

Christ Got Up, an Easter Reading

Chapter Twenty

The following essay was written by William H. Willimon, in his book *A Will to Lead, and the Grace to Follow*:

Doing Something Different

1. We were in church, following the order of worship like always, when Christ got up and left with the mumbled words; "I'm sick of what you've done to Sunday, I'm doing Easter."
2. We were just having a meeting plodding through the agenda, when Christ got up and headed for the door. "This is boring," we heard him say as he headed out.
3. We were just being church, involved in a community mission outreach program, helping people in need, when Christ sighed, groaned, and got up saying, "I need air."
4. We were wilting, sagging, wearing down, ready to throw in the towel, when Christ got up and with a smirk said, "I'm going to start [a protest movement. Anyone want to join the march?]"
5. We were just settling in at our retreat location, getting to know one another, feeling safe and secure when Christ got up and shouted, "I am the way, and the truth, and the life. Follow me!"
6. We were just nicely into our small group trying to understand the Biblical significance for daily living, when Christ got up, slammed the book shut, saying, "Let's do it rather than talk about it."
7. We were just sealing him away in the tomb, with the gravestone in place, adjusting to life without him, getting used to death and defeat, when Christ got up, kicked the stone away, came up and said, "Get up, let's start a church."
8. The denominational executive decided to move a young pastor into a church that had been dying for years. The Area minister protested that the church was really dead with no hope. The denominational executive said, "I'll report that to the young pastor, but I warn you, this guy really believes that Easter is true. He just sees death as an opportunity to see what Jesus can do." Let's get up![39]

---

39   William H. Willimon, *A Will to Lead, and the Grace to Follow* (Nashville, TN: Abingdon Press, 2011), 26–28.

Least Bittern (Deuteronomy 6:5)

Dialogue with Silence
Chapter Twenty-One

Thomas Merton joined a Trappist monastery in the United States to fulfil his vows of silence, prayer, and quiet contemplation. His writings then became so popular that he toured the world until his death at age fifty-three. His focus here is on Christ and His cross, to the exclusion of all else. It is an excellent Communion meditation.

My Lord, I have no hope but in your cross. You, by your humility, suffering and death, have delivered me from all vain hope. You have killed the vanity of the present life in yourself and have given me all that is eternal in rising from the dead.

My hope is in what the eye has never seen. Therefore let me not trust in visible rewards. My hope is in what the human heart cannot feel. Therefore let me not trust in the feelings of my heart. My hope is in what the hand has never touched. Do not let me trust what I can grasp between my fingers, because death will loosen my grasp and my vain hope will be gone.

Let me trust in your mercy, not in myself. Let my hope be in your love, not in health or strength or ability or human resources.

If I trust you, everything else will become for me strength, health and support. Everything will bring me to heaven.[40]

---

40 Thomas Merton, *Dialogue with Silence: Prayers and Drawings*, ed. Johnathon Montaldo (San Francisco, CA: HarperCollins, 2001), 109.

Red-Tailed Hawk (Psalm 19:1)

Readings on Healing and Forgiveness

Chapter Twenty-Two

While compiling this book, I felt that it would be important, for the worship of God's people, to include some scriptural reference for the Lord's Supper. The following verses provide such a focus.

He said, "If you listen carefully to the Lord your God and do what is right in his eyes, if you pay attention to his commands and keep all his decrees, I will not bring on you any of the diseases I brought on the Egyptians, for I am the Lord, who heals you."

—Exodus 15:26, NIV

How blessed is he whose transgression is forgiven, whose sin is covered! How blessed is the man to whom the Lord does not impute iniquity, and in whose spirit there is no deceit!… I acknowledged my sin to You, and my iniquity I did not hide; I said, "I will confess my transgressions to the Lord"; and You forgave the guilt of my sin.

—Psalm 32:1–2, 5

Bless the Lord, O my soul, and all that is within me, bless His holy name. Bless the Lord, O my soul, and forget none of His benefits; who pardons all your iniquities, who heals all your diseases; who redeems your life from the pit, who crowns you with lovingkindness and compassion; who satisfies your years with good things, so that your youth is renewed like the eagle.

—Psalm 103:1–5

Surely our griefs He Himself bore, and our sorrows He carried; yet we ourselves esteemed Him stricken, smitten of God, and afflicted. But He was pierced through for our transgressions, He was crushed for our iniquities; the chastening for our well-being fell upon Him, and by His scourging we are healed.

—Isaiah 53:4–5

Readings on Healing and Forgiveness

When evening came, they brought to Him many who were demon-possessed; and He cast out the spirits with a word, and healed all who were ill. This was to fulfill what was spoken through Isaiah the prophet: "He Himself took our infirmities and carried away our diseases."

—Matthew 8:16–17

If we confess our sins, He is faithful and righteous to forgive us our sins and to cleanse us from all unrighteousness.

—1 John 1:9

And if anyone sins, we have an Advocate with the Father, Jesus Christ the righteous; and He Himself is the propitiation for our sins; and not for ours only, but also for those of the whole world.

—1 John 2:1–2

Is anyone among you in trouble? Let them pray. Is anyone happy? Let them sing songs of praise. Is anyone among you sick? Let them call the elders of the church to pray over them and anoint them with oil in the name of the Lord. And the prayer offered in faith will make the sick person well; the Lord will raise them up. If they have sinned, they will be forgiven.

—James 5:13–15, NIV

Is not the cup of blessing which we bless a sharing in the blood of Christ? Is not the bread which we break a sharing in the body of Christ? Since there is one bread, we who are many are one body; for we all partake of the one bread.

—1 Corinthians 10:16–17

For as often as you eat this bread and drink the cup, you proclaim the Lord's death until He comes.

—1 Corinthians 11:26

The Blessing

Mute Swan (Psalm 51:7)

An Atheist Tells Us How to Win Others to Christ

Chapter Twenty-Three

Pastor Scott Sauls represents the softer and winsome side of the Christian faith. Instead of confrontation, he seeks consensus and agreement over differences that don't really matter in the end. And in his approach to discipleship and witnessing to the non-Christian, he wants us to get closer to the stranger and get to know him as a friendly person who might be interested in knowing more about our Saviour and theirs.

1. Be like Jesus: hang with sinners and judge the judgers.
2. Form genuine relationships with people, don't treat them as projects.
3. Actions speak louder than words.
4. When talking about religious and philosophical matters, ask more questions, and do less preaching.
5. Don't give unsolicited advice or judgments. Support people and wait for them to ask for your input if they want it.
6. Appreciate that nominal Christians are Christians too.
7. Don't try to force others into Christian participation.
8. Understand atheists and embrace the opportunity confrontational atheists afford you.
9. Respect other religions even as you evangelize their members. The light is there if they follow it.
10. Love your enemies not just your tribe.[41]

---

[41] Scott Sauls, *Jesus Outside the Lines: A Way Forward for Those Who Are Tired of Taking Sides* (Carol Stream, IL: Tyndale House, 2015), 195–197.

The Blessing

Red-Necked Grebe (John 1:16)

The Tradition of the Communion

Chapter Twenty-Four

As it pertains to the Lord's Supper, here are ten principles which it is important for Christians to stand on.

1. Tradition. Before anything was written about the life and teachings of Jesus, the Lord's Supper was already being practiced. This was based on Jesus's own institution of it (1 Corinthians 11:23–26, Acts 2:42)
2. Together. It began not as an individual or isolated event but a gathering of the people of God in one place to celebrate Jesus's death for them.
3. Thanksgiving. Jesus gave thanks to the Father for the bread and the cup, symbols of His body and blood. We also give thanks for both before partaking.
4. Thoughts. We are to think about Christ—His person, passion, promises, and place now. Our own self-examination is also a part of our thinking.
5. Taking. We take and eat, and take and drink, in remembrance of Christ's sacrifice and finished work of redemption on the cross.
6. Testimony. Through the Lord's Supper, we testify or give evidence that we believe in the Lord Jesus Christ as our personal Saviour and Lord. Indeed, if the pulpit or anything else does not preach the Saviour, the table does!
7. Trust. The words *"until He comes"* (1 Corinthians 11:26) mean that we make a promise and commitment to continue this tradition until the Lord Jesus returns the second time in power and great glory.
8. Table. A table is the designated furniture for observing the Lord's Supper in most churches. It is not to be an altar, as in the Old Testament, since the sacrifice of Jesus was accomplished once for all (Hebrews 10:10–14).
9. Timing. The words *"as often as you drink it"* (1 Corinthians 11:26) mean that you drink regularly or repeatedly as a congregation. The Baptist norm is a monthly remembrance led by deacons and pastors.
10. Test. Do we love Christ and each other? The Communion is a test.

The Blessing

Sandhill Crane (Job 39:13)

Beginning Thoughts on Communion

Chapter Twenty-Five

The Lord's Supper, also known as Communion, began as a celebration of the Passover meal to remember Moses and the Exodus, including the plagues on the Egyptians. Jesus made it the beginning of the church. Some also call it the Eucharist, or simply breaking bread.

The practice is mentioned in the four gospels (Matthew 26:20–30, Mark 14:12–26, Luke 22:1–30, John 13:21–38). The apostle Paul also gives us an account of Jesus's revelation to him of the Supper (1 Corinthians 11:23–34). Therefore, as we gather together, we remember:

- His person—who Jesus was and how He showed Himself in His teaching, healing, miracles, and way of life.
- His passion—His betrayal, trial, beatings, crucifixion on the cross, death, burial, and resurrection.
- His promises—of His appearances for forty days, ascension to heaven, preparation, and return.
- His place—at the Father's right hand, praying for us, coming in power and great glory, and the judgment.
- His invitation—according to Paul, every believer is welcomed to partake in the table ceremony as often as it is offered by their church (1 Corinthians 11:23–34). This is to be done with reverence, reflection, and personal examination.
- His warning—there is a warning of discipline and temporary judgment from the Lord for wrong, erroneous, and undisciplined behaviour before and at the table. The biblical context for this warning is drunkenness and partiality between rich and poor believers. The key is to remember that the symbols of broken bread and poured out wine or grape juice represent the body and blood of the Lord Jesus Christ for us. And if weakness, sickness, and even death are possible for abuse, what can joyful observance bring but strength, health, life, and blessing?

I now offer a few final notes.

The Blessing

I believe no one has the right to decide who is welcomed to the Lord's Supper. We are to examine ourselves, not each other.[42]

I believe there are more positive reasons to partake of the Communion service than negative ones.

I believe that through His Holy Spirit, God can and does dispense any discipline required without our permission or interference. I believe this action to be temporal in this life, without eternal consequences.

I believe that when we stay away from the table for any reason, we miss out on whatever God in Christ has for us for that Sunday or any other time.

Pileated Woodpecker (Psalm 104:27)

---

42   Some terrible mistakes over the issue of "worthiness" have taken place in the history of the church, and perhaps even in our own experience!

Problems with Eating and Drinking the Elements

Chapter Twenty-Six

Many have problems with the part of eating and drinking the elements at the Lord's Table, which John describes (John 6:48–71). From the text, Jesus had been disputing with the Jews about the nature of the real bread they were to eat, comparing it to Moses and the manna eaten in the wilderness. He tried to explain that they had to partake of Him—His body and blood.

> *I am the living bread that came down out of heaven; if anyone eats of this bread, he will live forever; and the bread also which I will give for the life of the world is My flesh.*
>
> —John 6:51

They did not understand and continued to disagree, to the point of some of His disciples potentially withdrawing. But His definitive words make it plain:

> *Truly, truly, I say to you, unless you eat the flesh of the Son of Man and drink His blood, you have no life in yourselves. He who eats My flesh and drinks My blood has eternal life, and I will raise him up on the last day. For My flesh is true food, and My blood is true drink. He who eats My flesh and drinks My blood abides in Me, and I in him.*
>
> —John 6:53–56

He further spiritualized His meaning, *"It is the Spirit who gives life; the flesh profits nothing; the words that I have spoken to you are spirit and are life"* (John 6:63).

We need to be certain of Jesus's meaning here:

The Blessing

- Jesus did not there and then, nor at the last supper, nor on the cross, nor following the resurrection, tear His body into pieces and give parts to his followers.[43]
- He used symbolic language to say that they participated in His life through believing in Him and the work of the Holy Spirit.
- The elements of broken bread and wine or grape juice (or any other symbol used in an emergency) do not change the substance in our mouths and stomach. These are spiritual words with spiritual meaning.
- We partake of these earthly symbols in memory of what Jesus dying on the cross has done for us. Any other belief goes beyond what Jesus did and meant.
- But if we are mistaken in any way of celebration and remembering Jesus's death *"in an unworthy manner… [we] shall be guilty of the body and blood of the Lord… For he who eats and drinks, eats and drinks judgment to himself if he does not judge the body rightly"* (1 Corinthians 11:27, 29). Those who do so know what they do and suffer the Lord's discipline of weakness, sickness, and even death (1 Corinthians 11:30).
- Despite the warning, I believe this judgment and discipline is earthbound and not eternal in consequence—or else those Christian groups like the Quakers and Salvation Army, who do not celebrate the Supper in their meetings, would not get into heaven!

---

43   Note: After the resurrection, the bread which He shared with the two on the road to Emmaus, the broiled fish with the eleven, and the breakfast on the seashore with seven all proved that He had a physical body, changed but still intact!

Sora (Colossians 3:1)

Dry Bones, an Easter Story
Chapter Twenty-Seven

Ezekiel 37:1–14

There is a tradition at House for All, a church in southern California, whereby the congregation chants a psalm and then reads from the gospel, an epistle, and a Hebrew Bible text, all from the Anglican or Episcopalian prayer book.

But at the Great Vigil of Easter, traditionally there are twelve readings. The congregants gather around a candle once a year and "tell each other the great stories of our faith so that we can remember who we are."[44]

One Sunday, a man named Stephen who looked like the combination between an aging movie star and Fortune 500 vice president, wanted to do the Valley of the Dry Bones reading from Ezekiel.

When Stephen walked up with a single sheet of paper, the light bouncing off his perfect head of salt-and-pepper hair, he said that he felt emotionally dead and that for this condition, nothing makes a difference:

No website; no relationship; no Mac computer or iPhone; no exercise, no diet, no supplement; no job, office, or title on my business card; no amount of diet Coke, good scotch, or bad beer; no self-help book, therapist, or self-improvement class; no car, house, or any other status symbol I can think to buy; no movie or video game.

They have all done nothing more than temporarily anesthetize (freeze) the longing in my soul to be complete, to be whole, to be connected, to be okay, to love and be loved as I am now with too much weight, too much debt, too much depression, too much gray, too much geek, and not enough of everything else.

And I despair that my trip on this rock, flying around the sun at sixty-seven thousand miles an hour, is just some sort of sick cosmic joke.

But then I remember. I remember the Valley. The Valley of the Dry Bones.

---

44 Nadia Bolz-Weber, *Acclaimed Saints: Finding God in All the Wrong People* (San Francisco, CA: Random House, 2015), 149.

Dry Bones, an Easter Story

God is talking to the prophet Ezekiel and guides him into something resembling a massive open grave. It is a valley covered, from one end to the next, with nothing but humanity at its core–dry bones. In this valley there is absolutely no hope of life.

God tells Ezekiel to cry out, cry out to those dry bones, cry out to God's children. Tell them to rise, tell them to rise, tell them to listen to God and rise. They listen.

And God lifts them up, puts them back together, and breathes into them. And they breathe anew. And God fills them with the Spirit. And where there was once death, hopelessness, and despair, there is new life.

In hearing that, there is light. There is hope.

And that is sufficient.[45]

Stellar Jay (Psalm 104:21)

---

45 Ibid., 147–149.

The Imitation of Christ
Chapter Twenty-Eight

Following the church split of the Middle Ages, when most of the world was experiencing a chaos of leadership, Thomas à Kempis wrote his classic devotional work *The Imitation of Christ*. He left it behind when he died in 1471 at the age of ninety-one, having served as a monastic monk for most of his life.

Of the four sections of this work, or "books," the last fifty pages are devoted to the Lord's Supper—or, as he called it, the Sacrament. Most of the chapters are filled with deep devotion, wise counsel, and exhortations to humility and meekness, while revealing his own loving heart for his Saviour.

Thomas took several pages to share his patience in seeking the Lord in the Sacrament, and in this sample compared himself to four Old Testament characters. I paraphrase the essence of his dialogue with his disciple:

Noah took 100 years to make an ark to save such a small number, how can I prepare my soul for the Sacrament in just an hour or less?

Moses—If Moses made an ark of the covenant to contain the law after 40 days on the mountain, how can I pray for just one hour before taking the Sacrament from the maker of all things?

Solomon—If the king of Israel took seven years to build the temple to praise the Lord in, and took eight days to dedicate it, how can I a poor sinful creature receive you into my house?

David—If David composed psalms to sing and praise God, we therefore ought with much reverence and devotion receive the body and blood of the Saviour.[46]

Thomas likewise challenges our modern focus on things other than the cross of Jesus:

Jesus has now many lovers of His heavenly kingdom, but few bearers of His cross.

He has many that are desirous of consolation, but few of tribulation.

He has many companions of His table, but few of His abstinence.

---

46 Thomas à Kempis, *Of the Imitation of Christ*, trans. Abbot Justin McCann (New York, NY: New American Library, 1957), 156–157.

All desire to rejoice with Him, but few are willing to endure anything for His sake.

Many follow Jesus to the breaking of bread, but few to the drinking of the chalice of His passion.

Many reverence His miracles, but few follow the shame of His cross.

Many love Jesus as long as they meet with no adversity; many praise Him and bless Him as long as they receive some consolations from Him.

But if Jesus hide himself and leave them for a little while, they either murmur or fall into excessive dejection.

But, if men love Jesus for Jesus' sake, and not for the sake of some consolation of their own, they bless Him no less in tribulation and anguish of heart than in the greatest consolation.

And though He should never give them consolation, yet would they always praise Him, and always give Him thanks. O how powerful is the pure love of Jesus, when mixed with no self-interest or self-love.[47]

And He is very certain what taking the Sacrament does for him. It is:

the health of soul and body, the medicine of every spiritual malady. By it my vices are cured, my passions restrained, my temptations overcome or lessened; greater grace is infused, incipient virtue increased, faith confirmed, hope strengthened and charity enkindled and enlarged.[48]

---

47 Ibid., 66.
48 Ibid., 163.

The Blessing

Great Horned Owl (Psalm 102:6)

Who to Choose

Chapter Twenty-Nine

Israel, both as a nation and people, was going through terrible times during the prophet Ezekiel's ministry. They faced exile to Babylon and were inflamed by the prospects of famine, wild beasts, plague, and sword.

God told them, through Ezekiel, that there was no escape:
"…even though these three men, Noah, Daniel and Job *were in its midst, by their own righteousness they could only deliver themselves," declares the Lord God.*

—Ezekiel 14:14 (emphasis added)

Ezekiel was so emphatic about this declaration that it got repeated four times in seven verses. Each time, the four judgments to come were also repeated: sword, famine, wild beasts, and plague (Ezekiel 14:14–21).

In seeking to ponder why these three men—Noah, Daniel, and Job—were the most worthy and righteous, here are some thoughts on each.

- Noah was chosen for his persevering preaching, for one hundred years, during an evil age in preparing the ark (2 Peter 2:5).
- Daniel was chosen for his righteous prayer life and interpretation of dreams before King Nebuchadnezzar of Babylon, without compromising his spiritual allegiance to the God of Israel (Daniel 2:28–49).
- Job was chosen for his patient endurance through his suffering trials and privations (James 5:11).

Therefore, it does seem that God is aware of the state and condition of our spiritual lives and honours, among other things, faith, righteous living, devotion, patience, perseverance, suffering, extreme and isolating loneliness, the prospect of facing opposition against all odds, even in the face of certain death.

Who would you choose?

The Blessing

I have thought that deliverance for each of these men was promised and secure. One might even suggest other examples of biblical types where similar scenarios took place:

- Enoch was translated so that he did not experience death (Genesis 5:21–24, Hebrews 11:5).
- Moses supposedly died of old age at one hundred twenty, but there was no funeral because God hid his body, then transfigured him along with Elijah to appear with Jesus at His transfiguration while preparing for His exit on the cross (Matthew 17:1–8).
- Elijah was raptured, or taken away in a chariot of fire, and later appeared with Jesus and Moses on the Mount of Transfiguration (2 Kings 2:1–12).
- Jesus transfigured, or changed, to appear in glorious splendour with Moses and Elijah on the Mount of Transfiguration (Luke 9:28–36).

For those who are serious about their devotion to their Saviour Jesus, this is part of the ascent to the hill of the Lord. If God can do this for the above mentioned characters of His choosing, what more would He be able to do *"abundantly beyond all that we ask or think, according to the power that works within us"* (Ephesians 3:20).

Virginia Rail (Hebrews 4:16)

Who May Ascend?
Chapter Thirty

Finally, the psalmist asked in Psalm 24:3, *"Who may ascend…?"* And what is the blessing to be received by one who ascends? It is something given by God as a reward, and certain requirements are attached. It is something God gives and no man can take away.

There are, however, some protocols associated with this ascent which we must be aware of.

1. Someone else is number one. As Psalm 24:1–2 tells us, *"The earth is the Lord's, and all it contains, the world, and those who dwell in it. For He has founded it upon the seas and established it upon the rivers."* This might be a tough one for modern twenty-first-century seekers to handle. God is the boss!

2. Someone else is king of the hill. This literally is true! God decides who comes up higher and on what terms. So who may ascend? Who may stand?

The answer, according to Psalm 24:4, is *"he who has clean hands and a pure heart."* That's the positive. The negative is he *"who has not lifted up his soul to falsehood and has not sworn deceitfully."*

These attributes of character are not out of reach except for the chosen few, or else why would God tease us? These are pursuits that seem within the possibility of the heart of he who yearns for more of the Lord. So don't lie to God. Be honest. Act uprightly. Keep your promises. Be open to whatever and wherever the Lord leads.

After all, Jesus said that everything rests on these two summary commandments: love God and love your neighbour (Matthew 22:36–40). He further promised,

> *Come to Me, all who are weary and heavy-laden, and I will give you rest. Take My yoke upon you and learn from Me, for I am gentle and humble in heart, and you will find rest for your souls. For My yoke is easy and My burden is light.*
>
> —Matthew 11:28–30

And His beloved John wrote,

The Blessing

> *For this is the love of God, that we keep His commandments; and His commandments are not burdensome.*
> —1 John 5:3 (emphasis added)

What is His reward then?

1. Someone else passes around the rewards. Blessing comes from the Lord, and righteousness comes from God for salvation.

2. Someone else manages the line-up for these coveted prizes. And by the grace of God, there are still those who seek this kind of relationship with God. A whole generation, in fact!

> *He shall receive a blessing from the Lord and righteousness from the God of his salvation. This is the generation of those who seek Him, who seek Your face—even Jacob.*
> —Psalm 24:5–6

By way of speculation, could this be a picture of Israel returning as a nation and people to God in the last days (Romans 9–11)? Both Isaiah and Ezekiel speak of this:

> *Can a land be born in one day? Can a nation be brought forth all at once?*
> —Isaiah 66:8

> *…I will gather them from every side and bring them into their own land… and they will all have one shepherd.*
> —Ezekiel 37:21, 24

The psalmist concludes with a double request of entrance into the city, with the lifting up of the gates by the King of glory:

> *Who is this King of glory? The Lord strong and mighty, the Lord mighty in battle… He is the King of glory.*
> —Psalm 24:8, 10

There need not be much of a stretch of the imagination to suggest that the King of glory is Christ the Messiah, but He is also the strong and mighty warrior knocking on the ancient doors for entrance to claim His throne and kingdom. And all who follow in His train, be they prisoners in submission, worshipers in rejoicing, citizens welcoming the victorious king home from battle, Gentile or Jew, bond or free, rich or poor, male or female, young or old… all are a part of the entourage of the victor, Jesus Christ the Lord of glory! Amen.

Finally, we come again to this verse and question: *"Who may ascend into the hill of the Lord? And who may stand in His holy place?"* (Psalm 24:3). This may be a key to open the door of great blessing and possibilities from the Lord! How can this be?

Consider this story from Duncan Campbell, who was leading revival meetings on the Islands of Lewis and Skye off the coast of Scotland in 1949.

Two elderly sisters, aged eighty-two and eighty-four, and a number of men had been praying for several months for revival to come to their parish… and nothing happened.

One morning, a young man in their company read to the others this exact text from Psalm 24: "Who may ascend into the hill of the Lord? And who may stand in His holy place? He who has clean hands and a pure heart… He shall receive a blessing from the Lord." Looking down on his praying companions, and speaking in Gaelic, he added, "Brethren, it seems to me so much sentimental humbug to be praying as we have been praying, to be waiting as we have been waiting here, if we ourselves are not rightly related to God. Are my hands clean, is my heart pure?"

He got no further. At that moment, there came to the people a realization of God, an awareness of His presence, that lifted them from the sphere of the ordinary into the sphere of the extraordinary. Three of them fell prostrate on the floor. Revival had come and the power that was let loose in that barn shook the whole community of Lewis and its surrounding area for the next three years.[49]

---

[49] Wesley L. Duewel, *Heroes of the Holy Life* (Grand Rapids, MI: Zondervan, 2002), 22–38. See also: Andrew Woolsey, *Duncan Campbell: A Biography* (London, UK: Hodder & Stoughton, 1974).

The Blessing

Wood Duck (1 Corinthians 11:1)

Conclusion

In this era of pandemic and worldwide speculation, without being overly prophetic or fear-mongering, when everything is tried, is this too outlandish and out of this world? Is it a fantasy?

Are we the type to say, "Okay, thank you very much. It's business as usual. We'll just wait until this passes." Or is there something we're lacking that only God's Holy Spirit can supply?

Indeed, who may ascend into the hill of the Lord? Is this us, we, me, you? And what might this blessing look like in our spiritual lives and in the local church?

Consider this. Coldness would become warmth and welcome. Indifference would become friendship. Carelessness would become caring. A handshake would become a hug. Lip service would become loving service. Negatives would become positives. Relationships would be renewed, family units would be restored, and friction would become flow. No would become yes, and instead of leaving there would be lingering.

All of these things would become common—natural, not forced or pushed or programmed. There would be unity among the fellowship, acceptance, a willingness to belong and eagerness to serve with regret for missing anything that God's Holy Spirit is doing. Spiritual lives would grow, answers to prayer would come, and miracles would not be uncommon if and when God wills them. Salvation would happen regularly, holiness of life would become a reality, and Christian joy and the peace of God would follow like a river blessing everything it touches (Ezekiel 47:1–12).

Throughout this book, my son Christopher has given us images of birds bound by gravity to earth, but with wings to soar to the heavens and in a sense touch the face of God. Possibilities exist beyond our wildest dreams, but is anything impossible with God?

Consider this promise:

For every beast of the forest is Mine, the cattle on a thousand hills. I know every bird of the mountains, and everything that moves in the field is Mine. If I were hungry I would not tell you, for the world is Mine, and all it contains. Shall I

The Blessing

eat the flesh of bulls or drink the blood of male goats? Offer to God a sacrifice of thanksgiving and pay your vows to the Most High; call upon Me in the day of trouble; I shall rescue you, and you will honor Me.

—Psalm 50:10–15

Is there the feel and sense here of a touch of the mystical, the mysterious, the untouchable, or the unreachable? This is how the saintly Samuel Rutherford envisioned it from a prison cell:

Whoso looketh to the cross of Christ and can take it up handsomely with faith and courage, shall find it such a burden as sails are to a ship, or wings to a bird.[50]

Perhaps it is not too late to claim the promise of Isaiah:

Why would you ever complain, O Jacob, or, whine, Israel, saying, "God has lost track of me. He doesn't care what happens to me"? Don't you know anything? Haven't you been listening? God doesn't come and go. God lasts. He's Creator of all you can see or imagine. He doesn't get tired out, doesn't pause to catch his breath. And he knows everything, inside and out. He energizes those who get tired, gives fresh strength to dropouts. For even young people tire and drop out, young folk in their prime stumble and fall. But those who wait upon God get fresh strength. They spread their wings and soar like eagles, they run and don't get tired, they walk and don't lag behind.

—Isaiah 40:29–31, MSG

Bald Eagle (Isaiah 40:31)

---

[50] Eva S. Sandeman, *Daily Thoughts for a Year from the Letters of Samuel Rutherford* (Edinburgh, UK: Oliphant, Anderson & Ferrier), letter lxxi.

About the Author

Rev. Dr. Charles E. Jackson is a seasoned Baptist pastor who belongs to the over-forty club (i.e. forty years of ordained ministry). He was raised in a north end suburb of Toronto and was sent to a small outreach Sunday school called Wilson Avenue Baptist Church, where they had a Bible Gold Miners Club on Friday nights for areas kids. He was one of the troublemakers who spent his nickel offering on candy before he got there!

But something must have gotten through by the Holy Spirit, because he remembered that God loved him, that Jesus had died for him, and that he needed a Saviour. The two teachers who sang, played the piano, and faithfully taught the gospel at that mission church attended his ordination service more than twenty-five years later.

But it took more work before he raised his hand for prayer at an evening service where Dr. A.W. Tozer was preaching. The invitation hymn went like this, based on Isaiah 1:18: "Whiter than snow. Yes, whiter than snow. Now wash me and I shall be whiter than snow."

It worked, the Word stuck, and the Holy Spirit did his work. Charles was baptized, became a member of the Avenue Road Alliance Church (now Bayview Glen), became a deacon, and then the captain of the Christian Service Brigade.

A handful of the young converts from that church ended up attending Toronto Bible College (now Tyndale University), where Charles graduated and looked to serve the Lord on the mission field, or on the home front in the pastorate.

Charles was directed to a small Baptist pastorate in Queensville, near Newmarket, where he preached twice every Sunday, taught the young people, and led the weekly prayer and Bible study. He worked full-time during this period at the Borough of North York (now part of the City of Toronto) and also managed to gain credits toward a bachelor's degree at the new Atkinson College (now part of York University).

His next move came at the urging of a family doctor, who asked him to consider Christian education at a large midtown Toronto church, Yorkminster Park Baptist Church. This challenging work encompassed all aspects of ministry except preaching and pastoral care, which were capably covered by suitably honoured doctoral clergy.

At its height, this church listed 1,200 members.

After a five-year period of building in the area of Christian education, Charles felt the need to preach in his own pastoral setting and accepted a call to an inner city parish in the east end of Toronto: Woodbine Heights Baptist Church. A highlight of this ministry was setting up a summer day camp for area children and young people who enjoyed very little by way of social interaction in a Christian setting.

This six-year pastorate then led Charles to Guelph and a larger congregation where the town-and-gown professionals held sway. Subsequent pastoral moves brought him to Kincardine and Lakefield, where he officially retired.

Now, almost fifteen years later, he is still ministering part-time, full-time, and in an interim capacity. He is also writing another book for publication.[51]

And what is it all for? This is the next part of the story.

Every believer in Christ seeks to be more like Jesus as they mature and grow in their Christian faith. For most, this involves a variety of spiritual disciplines, such as prayer, Bible reading and study, worship services, fellowship with other Christians, small group discussions, stewardship, and some form of service or outreach within the local church or outside it. This small offering seeks to provide spiritual food for the hungry soul. It can also be used as a resource for those who seek an answer to the psalmist's plea: who may ascend into the hill of the Lord?

The idea for this collection came out of monthly devotional thoughts for the Lord's Supper at First Baptist Church in Oshawa. Gathered over a period of a few years, it is hoped that this book contains some promptings of the Holy Spirit to urge readers to want more of what the Lord has for all of us.

May the Lord Jesus bless you as you read and think about your spiritual growth and journey, and may God be praised in all things.

---

51   His other two books include *The Burden* and *The Battle*.

About the Photographer

It is my pleasure to introduce my son, Christopher A. Jackson, who has honed an expertise over fifteen years in nature photography, specializing in avian photography both locally and internationally.

    Chris has captured images of many different species of birds, a limited number of which are presented throughout this book. A few pictures of other animals and creatures also appear.

    If you wish to contact Chris regarding any images you may be interested in, he can be reached at the following email address: jacksonca0823@gmail.com

    Chris will also consider requests for use of his images on a limited basis for purposes of presentation, conservation, and or education.

    Thank you, Chris.

Rev. Dr. Charles E. Jackson and Christopher A. Jackson

Index

Alaskan Black Bear ... 37
American Bittern. ... 6
Bald Eagle ... 72
Belted Kingfisher ... 10
Common Golden Eye ... 12
Common Merganser ... 14
Cooper's Hawk ... 16
Eastern Chipmunk ... 18
Four-Spotted Skimmer ... 20
Great Blue Heron ... 22
Great Horned Owl ... 64
Grey Jay (Canada's Official Bird) ... cover
Hooded Merganser ... 26
Horned Grebe ... 28
Least Bittern ... 45
Leopard Frog ... 34
Mink ... 3
Mute Swan ... 50
Northern Saw-Whet Owl ... 41
Osprey ... 43
Pileated Woodpecker ... 56
Red Fox ... 39
Red-Necked Grebe ... 52
Red-Tailed Hawk ... 47

The Blessing

Sandhill Crane 54
Snowy Owl 8, 30
Sora 59
Stellar Jay 61
Twelve-Spotted Skimmer 24
Virginia Rail 66
Wood Duck 70